REAL-LIFE
ZOMBIES

EDGE
BOOKS

BRAIN EATERS

CREATURES
WITH
ZOMBIELIKE DIETS

BY ALICIA Z. KLEPEIS

CAPSTONE PRESS
a capstone imprint

Edge Books are published by Capstone Press,
1710 Roe Crest Drive, North Mankato, Minnesota 56003
www.mycapstone.com

Cataloging-in-Publication Data is on file with the Library of Congress.
ISBN 978-1-5157-2479-7 (library binding)
ISBN 978-1-5157-2506-0 (eBook PDF)

Editorial Credits
Abby Colich, editor; Kyle Grenz, designer; Pam Mitsakos, media researcher;
Laura Manthe, production specialist

Photo Credits
Alex Wild Photography: Alex Wild/alexanderwild.com, 13; Getty Images: SCIENCE
SOURCE, 24-25 background; Science Source: D.P. Wilson/FLPA, 10, London School
of Hygiene & Tropical Medicine, 19; Shutterstock: Andrey_Kuzmin, 22-23 top
middle, ArCaLu, 7, ArtHeart, 25 middle left, Audrey Snider-Bell, 1 bottom middle,
corlaffra, 7 background, decade3d-anatomy online, back cover, dp Photography, 17,
dragon_fang, 18, Giovanni Cancemi, 29, graphit, 5, Hein Nouwens, 4, Horoscope,
cover, 26-27, John A. Anderson, 11, Juan Gaertner, 20, Kateryna Kon, 22-23
background, M. Cornelius, 9 background, Maksimilian, 6, Mikhail Blajenov, 26
middle, NancyS, 8-9 bottom middle, Olga Markova, 16, Rednex, 24 middle right,
reptiles4all, 14-15, Siriporn Schwendener, 12, vetpathologist, 28, Yuttapol Phetkong,
21

Design Elements: Shutterstock

Printed in the United States of America.
009680F16

TABLE OF CONTENTS

BINGING ON BRAINS

Deep inside a cave, a bat is fast asleep. A bird flies into the cave. The bird has a craving—for brains.

It finds its victim—the sleeping bat. The bird pecks viciously at the bat and drags it outside. The bird attacks its victim even more. Soon the bird reaches the bat's brain. The bird slurps up the brain. Is this killer bird a zombie? No. It's a great tit in the caves of Hungary.

From old legends to modern movies, zombies rise from the dead, hungry for human flesh. Brains are their favorite food. Even though human zombies aren't real, many creatures in nature enjoy a brain-filled diet. Brains provide many **nutrients** to hungry animals. Some **parasites** invade human brains. Although rare, they can cause many life-threatening illnesses and even death.

Binging on brains may be gross. But for some creatures, it's just another meal!

FAST FACT The idea of zombies eating brains began with the 1985 film *The Return of the Living Dead.* Earlier movies showed zombies eating human flesh, not brains in particular.

nutrient—a substance, such as a vitamin, that plants and animals need for good health

parasite—an animal or plant that lives on or inside another animal or plant

BRAIN-EATING BIRDS

Have you ever been sound asleep and woken up suddenly? At least you weren't awoken by a bird pecking at your head.

This real-life nightmare happens deep in the Bükk Mountains in northeastern Hungary.

Pipistrelle bats **hibernate** for the winter inside caves. Flocks of great tit birds hang out near these caves. The birds normally eat insects, but those are scarce in the winter. The great tits fly slowly into the cave. The bats wake up. They start uttering calls. Unfortunately, these calls may help the hungry birds more easily find their **prey** in the dark cave. The birds peck at the captured bats inside the cave. Sometimes they carry their prey out of the cave and into nearby trees. The tits peck and peck at the bats some more. Soon they reach the bats' brains. They remove the brains and eat up.

It's a zombie feast!

hibernate—to spend winter in a deep sleep; animals hibernate to survive low temperatures and lack of food

prey—an animal hunted by another animal for food

BRAIN-GOBBLING COLLARED PIKAS

Below the rocky Gulf of Alaska, the seas are icy. In these bleak conditions live zombielike creatures. These creatures will trick you. Collared pikas have the face of a teddy bear. But they have a disgusting secret.

These cuddly-looking critters eat bird brains!

FAST FACT Pikas belong to a group of mammals called lagomorphs. Almost all of the pika's lagomorph relatives, such as rabbits and hares, eat only plants.

Some plants grow in the area, but not enough to keep pikas full. So some pikas survive by taking advantage of other animals' misfortunes. Songbirds often fly through the area. Sometimes the birds get caught in storms. Winds from these storms smash the tiny birds against huge glaciers. The birds often die. Others fall to the ice exhausted.

Pikas fetch the dead birds. They gnaw tiny holes in the backs of the birds' heads. Then they eat the bird's brains. The brains are high in fat and **protein**. Pikas even store some bird bodies inside their hay piles. They snack on the stock through the winter.

protein—a chemical made by animal and plant cells to carry out various functions

SEA SQUIRTS
EAT THEIR OWN
BRAINS

At the bottom of the ocean lies an interesting creature. It has no eyes, no ears, and no fins. It's stuck to the seafloor, flapping as the water moves. This animal doesn't even have a brain! Why?

This critter, known as a sea squirt, ate its own brain!

sea squirt larva

A sea squirt's brain is much simpler than a human's. It's more like a network of **cells**. As a young **larva**, a sea squirt cannot eat. It sticks itself to a spot on the seafloor. It will live in this spot for the rest of its life. Once it is settled, the animal absorbs all the parts of its body that it doesn't need anymore. This includes the tail, gills, and its simple brain.

Talk about losing your mind!

The sea squirt continues to grow larger. It will spend the rest of its zombielike life sucking in water and filtering out food.

adult sea squirt

cell—a basic part of an animal or plant that is so small you can't see it without a microscope

larva—the stage of life of some animals between egg and adult

BRAIN-FEASTING PHORID FLIES

It's dusk in a rain forest in Brazil. A wounded ant lies on the ground. Soon a pair of phorid flies appears on the scene. They hover above the ant. The female fly moves in closer. She wants to be sure that the ant won't harm her. Otherwise, this tiny fly (smaller than the ant's head) could end up as the ant's dinner.

Luckily for the fly, the ant isn't moving.

Using her long mouthpart, the fly quickly cuts off the ant's head.

The fly flies away with her cargo. Sometimes the fly immediately chows down on the ant's head. Other times she lays eggs close by. When these eggs hatch, the larvae will have the ant head to feast on.

The Unusual Brain Eaters

For some animals brains are a part of their normal diets. Sometimes, though, witnesses spot some out-of-the-ordinary brain eating. Once in the Arizona desert, a Gila woodpecker varied from its usual meal of insects and fruit. For reasons unknown, it chose a more zombielike dinner—the brains of two baby mourning doves. You may have seen chipmunks carrying nuts and berries to their nests. But a few chipmunks have been spied munching on mice brains. Lumholtz's tree kangaroos in Australia reportedly sometimes chow down on the brains of doves and turkeys.

Zombie or not, it's delicious dining indeed!

BIRDEATER OR BRAIN SLURPER?

The South American Goliath birdeater is the world's largest spider.

The Goliath birdeater measures 1 foot (0.3 meter) across. It can weigh more than 6 ounces (170 grams). That's about the size of a newborn puppy! But despite its name, this terrifying tarantula doesn't often eat birds. Instead it eats nearly anything it finds on the ground. Usually it's earthworms. Sometimes it's the brains of a rodent or frog.

The birdeater lies in wait in its home on the forest floor. A mouse scurries by. The spider springs into action. It pierces the mouse's skull with its 0.75-inch (2-centimeter) long fangs. It then injects the mouse with venom. This venom starts dissolving the insides of the mouse. Then the spider gobbles down what's left of the brain and other innards.

FAST FACT Local people enjoy eating Goliath birdeaters. Some say these spiders taste like shrimp. After this snack people use the spider's long fangs as toothpicks. They remove any leftover spider bits from their teeth!

BRAIN-HUNGRY HUMANS

fried pork brains

Around the globe people eat brains too! Humans have been eating animal brains since the caveman days.

In many countries people consider animal brains a special treat.

Indian chefs cook goat brain curries. German cooks whip up a pot of *Hirnsuppe*, or calf brain soup. Mexican chefs might prepare cow brain tacos. Some folks in Indonesia eat monkey brains. They believe them to be healthy. African and Chinese chefs also cook with monkey brains.

Does the thought of eating brains sound disgusting? Maybe you'd rather stick to peanut butter and jelly. Or maybe you are brave enough to be brain eater. If you want to give them a try, only eat brains from a restaurant. The chef will know how to safely prepare them. Otherwise, eating animal brains could make you sick.

FAST FACT Scientists discovered fossils in Kenya that show our human ancestors ate antelope brains around 2 million years ago.

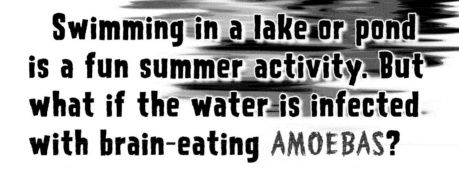

BRAIN-EATING AMOEBAS

Swimming in a lake or pond is a fun summer activity. But what if the water is infected with brain-eating AMOEBAS?

amoeba—a microscopic single-celled organism that lives in a wet environment

These amoebas live in warm lakes and ponds. They are found in water around 80 degrees Fahrenheit (27 degrees Celsius). Infected water can get up a person's nose. The amoebas then crawl into the brain. They begin eating right away.

An infected person may have a headache, fever, and nausea. Sometimes the victim's sense of smell changes. The amoebas cause swelling in the brain.

Beware of Brain Eaters

Keep yourself safe. Don't swim in water where these amoebas are known to live. If you go swimming in a place with warm, still water or in untreated hot springs, be sure to hold your nose with your thumb and finger. Or use a nose clip. You can also avoid putting your head in the water at all.

If untreated, the person can die.

Don't let this brain eater scare you. Millions of people each year swim in water where these amoebas live. Scientists aren't sure why only a few people become ill. In the United States, only three to four cases occur each year. There's about a one in 10 million chance you could get infected from swimming where these amoebas exist. There's no chance at all in a chlorinated swimming pool.

brain-eating amoebas

BRAIN-TASTING TAPEWORMS

Earthworms in the soil are good. Worms in your body are not. Tapeworms are parasites. Some tapeworms can live in the **intestines** of humans and other animals. One tapeworm, *Taenia solium*, can even reach the human brain.

Parasite Protection

Terrified of parasites getting into your body and eating your brain? Don't be. There are ways to protect yourself. Good hygiene will keep you safe from many illnesses. Always wash your hands well before preparing food and eating, and of course, after using the toilet. Make sure your meat is cooked thoroughly.

intestine—a long tube that carries and digests food and stores waste products

It starts when a person eats infected pork that hasn't been cooked through. Inside the pork are the tapeworm's eggs. The eggs end up in the person's intestines. When the person uses the toilet, the eggs come out with the poop. Then the person doesn't fully wash his or her hands. The eggs spread onto food or other surfaces the infected person touches. Other people swallow these eggs when eating food the infected person has made.

Once inside the second person, the eggs hatch. They grow into larvae. The larvae enter the person's blood. The blood carries the larvae through the person's body. They eventually reach the brain. Once inside the brain, these parasites form **cysts**. The cysts cause severe headaches. An infected person may have **seizures**. He or she can also develop **dementia** and swelling in the brain. A person may die if not treated.

Taenia solium tapeworm

cyst—a pouch or sac of fluid that develops inside the body, usually the result of disease or infection

seizure—a sudden attack that causes a person to shake violently

dementia—a brain condition that causes the inability to think, reason, or remember things

LITTER BOX BRAIN INVADERS

Look inside a litter box.
You'll see cat poop.

What you won't see are the eggs of the PROTOZOAN *Toxoplasma gondii* waiting to prey on a brain.

Cats can get this protozoan after eating an infected rat. The parasite comes out in the cat's poop. A person cleaning the cat's litter box may become infected. You can also get this parasite by eating undercooked meat or unwashed veggies grown in tainted soil.

protozoan—a tiny, microscopic animal

Some research suggests that this parasite can influence the personalities of those who carry it. For example, it may cause women to be more trusting. It may cause men to be more suspicious. Billions of people around the world could have their personalities affected by this tiny zombielike parasite!

Toxoplasma gondii is a common parasite. Scientists estimate one-third of people on Earth have it inside their brains. Most of them are perfectly healthy. Normally a person's **immune system** keeps him or her from getting sick from this parasite.

Sometimes this protozoan causes the disease toxoplasmosis. People have mild cold or flulike symptoms. Their brains become full of cysts. The parasite can break out from the cysts. Then it attacks the person's brain. This might cause the person to lose his or her eyesight. Other body functions may also be lost.

Is it your job to clean your cat's litter box? Don't worry. Most people don't get sick from the parasite.

Toxoplasma gondii
protozoa

Be sure to always wash your hands afterward.

immune system—the part of the body that protects against disease

MAD COW DISEASE

A cow staggers in a field, unsteady on its feet. Its movements are jerky. Its vision is blurred. Has this cow become a zombie? No. This animal is sick with mad cow disease.

In the 1980s cows in Great Britain were dying of a strange illness. The cows became aggressive. Some couldn't walk. Scientists soon discovered big clumps of protein in the animals' brains and spinal cords. This deadly protein came from the cows' feed. The feed contained ground-up brains of other cows and sheep. Holes formed in the infected cows' brains.

Mad cow disease made their brains look spongy, as if they'd been eaten away.

A few people who ate infected beef became sick. They experienced blurred vision, impaired thinking, and personality changes. The victims died within a year.

Don't fear your cheeseburgers! People cannot get this disease from drinking milk or eating milk products. No cases have been connected to beef eaten in the United States. Only 229 people worldwide have died from this disease.

FAST FACT In some parts of Kentucky, people dine on squirrel brains after hunting the animal. In 1997 a number of people who'd eaten them got a form of mad cow disease. Doctors then advised against chowing down on these furry creatures.

THE RABIES VIRUS

A raccoon crashes into a garbage can. Then it limps away. Its movements are jerky. It makes strange noises. It looks as if it's trying to bite an imaginary enemy. A stream of frothy spit drips from its mouth. This animal has the rabies **virus**.

How did the raccoon become a crazed critter?

virus—a germ that infects living things and causes diseases

Through the bite of another infected animal, such as a bat, the virus spread through saliva. From the bite, the virus traveled through the raccoon's body to the spinal cord and brain. Then it attacked the brain as it continued to spread.

People can get rabies if bitten by an infected animal. Rabies is not common in the United States. Only a few people die from rabies each year. If a wild animal or stray cat or dog bites you, go to the doctor right away. It's unlikely you have rabies. However, a doctor will know for sure if you need a shot to prevent the disease.

rabies virus

FLESH-EATING BACTERIA

In many stories zombies eat human flesh. Sound scary? Although rare, there are **bacteria** that do just that.

Victims of flesh-eating bacteria often have no idea how, when, or where they became ill. The bacteria can enter through a small insect bite or a tiny cut. Once the bacteria enter the body, they eat away at the skin. The bacteria cause the flesh to die. Flesh-eating bacteria spread fast.

If not treated quickly, the victim can die.

bacteria—single-celled, microscopic organisms that live everywhere in nature

skin affected by flesh-eating bacteria

Medicine sometimes helps stop the infection. The bacteria can kill so much flesh that doctors must remove it. Victims often lose limbs. Removal of flesh keeps the bacteria from spreading further through the body. Luckily, flesh-eating bacteria are rare. Doctors estimate fewer than 1,000 cases occur each year in the United States.

Did you think the world was safe from zombies? Now you know otherwise!

Zombies in movies might be fake, but brain eaters are alive and well in nature. Brain-eating organisms can also affect humans. Be sure to keep yourself healthy. Practice good hygiene and make sure your food is safe to eat.

bacteria that cause flesh-eating disease

GLOSSARY

amoeba (uh-MEE-buh)—a microscopic single-celled organism that lives in a wet environment

bacteria (bak-TEER-ee-uh)—single-celled, microscopic organisms that live everywhere in nature

cell (SEL)—a basic part of an animal or plant that is so small you can't see it without a microscope

cyst (SIST)—a pouch or sac of fluid that develops inside the body, usually the result of disease or infection

dementia (deh-MEN-chuh)—a brain condition that causes the inability to think, reason, or remember things

hibernate (HYE-bur-nate)—to spend winter in a deep sleep; animals hibernate to survive low temperatures and lack of food

immune system (i-MYOON SISS-tuhm)—the part of the body that protects against disease

intestine (in-TESS-tin)—a long tube that carries and digests food and stores waste products

larva (LAR-vuh)—the stage of life of some animals between egg and adult

nutrient (NOO-tree-uhnt)—a substance, such as a vitamin, that plants and animals need for good health

parasite (PAIR-uh-site)—an animal or plant that lives on or inside another animal or plant

prey (PRAY)—an animal hunted by another animal for food

protein (PROH-teen)—a chemical made by animal and plant cells to carry out various functions

protozoan (proht-uh-ZOE-uhn)—a tiny, microscopic animal

seizure (SEE-zhur)—a sudden attack that causes a person to shake violently

virus (VYE-ruhss)—a germ that infects living things and causes diseases

READ MORE

Goldsworthy, Steve. *Zombies: The Truth Behind History's Terrifying Flesh-Eaters.* Monster Handbooks. North Mankato, Minn.: Capstone Press, 2016.

Hirschmann, Kris. *Real Life Zombies.* New York: Scholastic Inc., 2013.

Johnson, Rebecca L. *Zombie Makers: True Stories of Nature's Undead.* Minneapolis, Minn.: Millbrook Press, 2013.

Larson, Kirsten W. *Zombies in Nature.* Freaky Nature. Mankato, Minn.: Amicus Ink, 2015.

INTERNET SITES

FactHound offers a safe, fun way to find Internet sites related to this book. All of the sites on FactHound have been researched by our staff.

Here's all you do:

Visit *www.facthound.com*

Type in this code: 9781515724797

Check out projects, games and lots more at
www.capstonekids.com

INDEX